# Eliza Fletcher

***Billionaire Daughter's jogger murder mystery***

***Sydney Walker***

## *Table Of Contents*

# INTRODUCTION

## *Who Is Eliza Fletcher?*

Ms. Fletcher had sought a career in teaching rather than teaming up with her family's firm which has developed into a tremendously successful multi-billion-dollar operation. Eliza Fletcher, 34, was out on her customary morning run near the University of Memphis when she vanished. Her family set up a $50,000 reward for information leading to the arrest of anybody guilty of her abduction after police indicated she had been abducted. Her corpse was recovered three days later.

She worked as a junior kindergarten teacher at St Mary's Episcopal School. The 34-year-old was married to Richard Fletcher III and they had two boys. Her grandfather, the late Joseph Orgill III, was a Memphis hardware magnate and philanthropist. Known to friends and family as "Liza,"

Fletcher was an accomplished runner and jogger, who ran the St. Jude marathon in Memphis with timing of 3:26:09. That time was quick enough time to qualify Fletcher for the Boston Marathon, one of the most elite marathons in the world. Out of all the ladies running the St. Jude marathon that year, she finished 22nd.

### *Where Is Eliza Fletcher From?*

She graduated from Hutchison School in Memphis in 2006, according to the all-website, girl's school's then would go on to earn a bachelor's degree in exercise and sports science at Baylor University and a master of art in teaching with an emphasis in elementary education at Belmont University, according to the Facebook post from St. Mary's.

### *Who Was Eliza's Husband?*

Described as "full of life" by George Robertson, the senior pastor of Second Presbyterian Church, Fletcher married Richard Fletcher III at the church in 2014. Then, the pair hosted their reception at the Dixon, Memphis Magazine said. They have two boys. "She and her husband Ritchie are both very active and great leaders in our congregation," Robertson said. "They have two small boys who have come up to me every week and given me a hug." "She and her husband are both inspirations in the sense of their enthusiasm for life and love of running and sports," Robertson added. "But what's most important at this time is they have really deep and genuine confidence in Christ, who they have depended on throughout their lives and who has had a very substantial influence on each of them individually. That is Ritchie's faith right now." Fletcher is the granddaughter of the late Joseph "Joe" Orgill III, Memphis hardware magnate and philanthropist who has sponsored initiatives like Dixon Gallery and Gardens and Church Health.

### *How did the family company become so successful?*

Despite coming from a wealthy background, Ms. Fletcher decided to pursue a career in teaching and not with her family's firm. Her late grandpa was a millionaire who supervised significant expansion in a Memphis hardware supply firm, known as Orgill. The firm is reported to be valued at more than $3bn (£2.6bn) and employs over 5,500 employees. Initially formed in 1847, it went through a succession of name and ownership changes until Joe Orgill III became company president in the late 1960s. The firm developed via the purchase of other companies and currently advertises itself as the "world's biggest independent hardlines distributor with annual sales exceeding $3 billion". According to the corporate website, it serves more than 11,000 retail shops, centers, and dealers across the US and Canada. It also distributes its services to stores in 50 other countries. Orgill states it is "celebrating 175 years" and has its headquarters in Collierville, Tennessee.

### *Liza Touched The Hearts Of Many*

Following her disappearance, her family made a video begging for aid in locating her. In the announcement, they also offered a $50,000 prize for information in the case. We feel someone knows what occurred and can assist, her uncle Mike Keeney said.

After the finding of her death, her family claimed they were "heartbroken and grieved" by their "senseless loss". "Liza has touched the hearts of many people," they said, describing her as "such a joy to so many". "Now it's time to remember and celebrate how exceptional she was and to support those who cared so much for her," the family statement stated. In a Facebook post, St. Mary's Episcopal School, where Fletcher taught kindergarten, said teachers and staff began Tuesday in the chapel and lit candles to remember her as "a brilliant light in our community".

Memphis Police Director Cerelyn "CJ," Davis said it was too early in the inquiry to identify how and where Fletcher was slain. Davis said the corpse was recovered behind an empty duplex. A police affidavit says investigators spotted car tracks near the duplex's driveway, and they "smelled a stench of rotting". Purple running shorts whose look was comparable with those Fletcher was wearing were recovered in a trash rubbish bag nearby, according to the affidavit.

# CHAPTER 1

## *Eliza Fletcher's Story*

Cleotha Abston, 38, has been accused of abduction and murder. But who was Eliza Fletcher, how did her family gain their billions, and what do we know about how she died? Memphis police officers examine an area where a corpse has been recovered in South Memphis, Tenn., between Victor Street and East Person Ave., Monday, Sept. 5, 2022. Police in Tennessee reported Tuesday, Sept. 6, that they have located the remains of a Memphis woman taken during a pre-dawn run, confirming suspicions that Eliza Fletcher was slain after she was forced into an SUV on Friday morning. Cleotha Abston has been accused of abduction and murder in the case. Abston, 38, is now facing accusations of first-degree murder and first-degree murder in perpetration of abduction. He was arrested by US Marshals on Saturday 3 September after his DNA was found on a pair of sandals near where Fletcher was last seen. Police also connected the car they suspect was used in the abduction to a person at a home where Abston was residing. Abston was previously sentenced to 24 years in prison for another crime.

He was barely 16 when he kidnapped a Memphis lawyer, Kemper Durand, in 2000. Mr. Durand was able to escape after several hours, and Abston was incarcerated after pleading guilty to exceptionally aggravated abduction and aggravated robbery. Abston pushed Mr. Durand into the trunk of his automobile at gunpoint. After many hours, Abston took Mr. Durand out and forced him to drive to a petrol station to take money from an ATM. Mr. Durand died in 2013 but he had indicated in a statement to the court that he was "very fortunate" to have been able to get away from Abston, adding: "It was quite possible that I would have been murdered had I not fled." According to Mr. Durand's testimony, Abston had previously been charged with a variety of crimes before his abduction, including serious assault with a weapon, and rape, some of which stretched back to when he was only 12. Abston did not complete his whole sentence and was freed after 20 years. Some prominent Tennessee Republicans were quick to argue that had Abston served his full sentence, Fletcher would still be alive.

The abduction and killing of Eliza Fletcher have captivated the attention of much of Memphis since she was last seen alive on Sept. 2. Since then, 38-year-old Cleotha Abston has been arrested and charged with first-degree murder and first-degree murder in perpetration of a kidnapping. Police said it appeared Abston acted alone. On September 4, 2022, Memphis police reported the arrest of a suspect, Cleotha Abston, a felon who was accused of abduction and is now facing first-degree murder and additional counts. Read more about him here. Abston, known as "Pookie" and "Wild," was recently freed from jail after being convicted in 2001 of kidnapping a Memphis defense attorney, who was put into the trunk of a car vehicle for two hours. Abston had published photographs of firearms on Facebook.

Authorities located Fletcher's corpse behind an empty apartment, they reported on September 6, 2022, completing a multi-day hunt that had captivated the city. The police chief said it was too early to ascertain the site and cause of death for Fletcher. In a press conference on September 6, Memphis police Chief C.J. Davis said, "Today is a very sad day in the city of Memphis." She expressed condolences to the family and friends impacted by the "heinous" kidnapping and murder of Fletcher. At 5:07 p.m. on September 5, police uncovered human remains at the back of a vacant duplex unit 1600 block of Victor Street. The corpse was subsequently conclusively identified as Fletcher, Davis said. Authorities characterized Fletcher as affecting many lives. The updated affidavit gave further alarming insights about Fletcher's death. It indicates that officials looked for Fletcher around East Person Avenue and Victor Street on September 5, 2022, according to data from the FBI. An officer noticed high grass south of a vacant residence, vehicle tracks in the grass, and smelled "an odor of decay."

Immediately to the right of the steps, the officer "located an unresponsive female lying on the ground."

About 100 feet north of 1591 S. Orleans Street, detectives located a discarded garbage bag that included the purple Lululemon shorts similar to the ones Fletcher was wearing to jog. Video analysis showed the suspect's car on the morning of the kidnapping between 5:48 a.m. and 5:52

a.m. going to several sites. Steven J. Mulroy, the District Attorney, claimed the murder was an "isolated act by a stranger," and that Fletcher's family was always cooperating with investigators. He read a letter from the family: "Please respect their privacy. Please allow them to mourn. At a suitable moment, they will be making a statement." The police statement describes a horrifying scenario in which Abston, 38, is accused of waiting for Fletcher to run past, then rushing her and pushing her into his car. He was afterward spotted washing the SUV. Cleotha Abston "declined to furnish investigators with the whereabouts of the victim," according to the affidavit. The affidavit characterizes the kidnapping as "violent," with the perpetrator, "waiting for, then rushing toward the victim." Authorities say, Fletcher, 34, "suffered substantial injury" that possibly left "evidence, e.g. blood, in the car that the defendant cleaned." Fletcher goes under the name Liza Fletcher on

Facebook, although officials supplied her identity as Eliza Fletcher.

### *Running In Fletcher's Honor*

Several thousand individuals have signed up to memorialize Fletcher in a memorial event dubbed "Finish Liza's Run" on Friday, Sept. 9. The run will start at 4:20 a.m. and take an 8.2-mile path that Fletcher would regularly run, starting near Central Ave. and Belvedere Street before cutting down Central to Zach Curlin Street and back towards Belvedere. "Our objective is to stand up for the ladies in the Mid South and underline that women should be allowed to safely run any time of day," the Facebook event page states. She hails from a renowned Memphis family, the granddaughter of a well-known philanthropist and business entrepreneur who died in 2018. The Daily Beast refers to her as a “billionaire’s granddaughter.”

# CHAPTER 2

## *Facts About The Billionaire's Granddaughter's Case*

**1. Police Have Charged Cleotha Abston With 'Especially Aggravated Kidnapping,' Saying He 'Aggressively' Rushed Fletcher':** The police affidavit reveals chilling details. It says they responded to a missing person report in the 1500 block of Carr Avenue at 7 a.m. September 2. Richard Fletcher advised that his wife went for her regular run around 4 a.m. and did not return home. At about 6:45 a.m., a citizen on a bike found her cellphone and a pair of men's Champion slides laying in the street in the same area. Investigators then obtained a video that showed a black GMC Terrain passing and then waiting for Fletcher to run by. A male exited the Terrain and "ran aggressively toward the victim," forcing her into the passenger's side of the vehicle after a struggle. The Champion slides were found in that area. The vehicle then sat in a parking lot, with the victim inside it, for about four minutes.

Police obtained a partial license plate number from another video, and they sent the Champion slides for DNA testing and got a hit in the CODIS database: Cleotha Abston (Henderson). Authorities then worked on confirming Abston's whereabouts "before, during, and after the abduction." They obtained surveillance footage of him wearing the same slides the day before the abduction at a Malco Theatre location. They found that he resided in the 5700 block of Waterstone Oak Way, a location with active utilities in the name of Gwendolyn Brown, who has a black 2013 GMC Terrain registered to her name. They also located a September 1, 2022, police report for Abston that listed his address at Waterstone Oak Way. The affidavit does not explain what that report was about.

The affidavit continues to allege that:
The owner of Majesty's Cleaning Service verified that she employed Abston and he drives a GMC Terrain.
Police determined Abston's cell phone was near the area where Fletcher was forced into the Terrain at the time of the abduction.
At 10:45 a.m. on September 3, 2022, the GMC Terrain was located by members of the U.S. Marshals Service.
Officers detained Abston when they saw him standing in a doorway. He tried to flee but was taken into custody.

A woman told police that she saw Abston at around 7:50 a.m. on the day of the abduction. He was at a different home — that of his brother, Mario Abston. He was cleaning the interior of the GMC Terrain with floor cleaner and "behaving oddly." Mario Abston stated that he saw Cleotha Abston cleaning the interior of the car with floor cleaner. Both also saw Abston washing his clothes in a sink in the house. Mario stated that Abston was "acting very strange." Police announced that Abston was charged in connection with Fletcher's disappearance on their Facebook page.

"The individual who was detained has been officially charged in connection with the abduction of Eliza Fletcher. At this point in the investigation, Cleotha Abston, 38, has been charged with Especially Aggravated Kidnapping and Tampering with Evidence," they wrote. "Eliza Fletcher has not been located at this time. MPD Investigators and officers, along with our local and federal partners, continue searching for Mrs. Fletcher." A second individual, currently not believed to be connected to Fletcher's abduction, was also arrested during this investigation. Mario Abston, 36, was charged with Possession of a Controlled Substance with Intent to Manufacture and Sell Fentanyl, Possession of a Controlled Substance with Intent to Manufacture and Sell Heroin, and Convicted Felon in

Possession of a Firearm During the Commission of a Dangerous Felony. This remains to be an active and ongoing investigation. We continue to ask for assistance from the community. If anyone has any information concerning this investigation, they should call CrimeStoppers at 901-528-CASH.

University of Memphis police said in a safety alert that Fletcher regularly "runs on Central Avenue," they wrote, and she was "reported missing after not returning home" at 7 a.m. Her "cell phone and water bottle were discovered in front of a house in the 3800 block of Central that is owned by the University." The phone was smashed, according to Action News 5. In a city watch alert, Memphis police characterized Eliza W. Fletcher, 34, as a "missing adult." "Victim went running early morning, was abducted, and forced into a mid-sized dark-colored SUV," police wrote. They said Fletcher is a white female, 5 foot 6 inches tall, 137 pounds, with brown hair, green eyes, hair in a bun, a pink jogging top, and purple running shorts. The suspect was described as an unknown male. People with information are encouraged to call the Memphis Police Department at 901-545-COPS (2677). Others have described her hair as blonde.

In a short news conference, Memphis police said that the University of Memphis called the Memphis Police Department, and initially they were "handling possibly a missing person." Police said in the news conference that they were not aware of a connection to a dark SUV harassing members of the University of Memphis women's cross country team. They also have not indicated any connection between Fletcher's abduction and the kidnapping of a young mother and child by gunpoint at a Memphis Target store on Wednesday. In that case, however, the victims were released after they withdrew $800 out of an ATM.

**2. Loved Ones Say, Liza Fletcher, a Teacher & Avid Runner, Qualified for the Boston Marathon & Was a College Athlete:** Her Family Spoke at a News Conference Before the Arrest. Fletcher's family held a news conference and spoke publicly about her abduction for the first time on September 3, 2022.

Fletcher's uncle read a statement, including from her husband, brother, and parents. Richie Fletcher and the other family members flanked the uncle. Fletcher is listed as a teacher at St. Mary's Episcopal School under the name Liza Fletcher. Her husband, Richie Fletcher III, works as a dealership manager for a Memphis boat center and was previously a Coast Guard mechanic, according to his LinkedIn page. The Fletchers have two small children. His full name is Richard Fletcher III. "We want to start by thanking everyone for their prayers and outpouring of support. Liza has touched the hearts of many people and it shows. We want to thank the Memphis Police Department, Shelby County Sheriff's Department, TBI, FBI, and all of the other law enforcement agencies who are working tirelessly to find Liza," the uncle said. "The family has met with the police and we have shared with them all the information we know. More than anything we want to see Liza return home safely. The family has offered a reward for any information that leads to her safe return. We believe someone knows what happened and can help. If you have any information on this crime or Liza's location, call the police at 901-545-COPS or CrimeStoppers, 901-528-CASH." journalist Ian Ripple reported, before Abston's arrest, that police had removed items from Fletcher's home. "Police are towing this vehicle from the home in the investigation of Eliza Fletcher's abduction. We also saw a computer and lawn shears tagged as evidence and removed from the home," he tweeted. Various items were marked as evidence, and a $50,000 reward is being offered, he reported. Family members asked for the community's help

In college, she played soccer for the University of Memphis. That bio says that Eliza, then Eliza Wellford, was born in Memphis, and it reads:

A four-year All-Region player who prepped at Hutchison School ... A four-time Commercial Appeal Best of Preps All-Metro Team selection and was the finalist for All-Metro Player of the Year in 2004 and 2005 ... All-state as a junior and senior ... Named the Most Valuable Player in 2003 ... Coached in high school by former Memphis soccer player Larry Creson ... Led school team to a 15-4-2 record as a senior ... Scored four goals against Collierville in 2005 ... Totaled 28 goals with five assists as a senior and 87 goals with 22 assists in her four years at Hutchison ... Play club soccer with the Memphis Mercury, coached by U of M assistant Jodi Grant ... Was a teammate of fellow Lady Tigers Brittany Baldwin and Lia Fannin ... Also a four-year letter winner in track and was named to The Commercial Appeal Best of Preps All-Metro team from 2001-05 ... Named the Outstanding Athlete at the Harding Relays in 2004 and was the pentathlon winner in 2004.

A friend wrote in a Facebook group devoted to finding Fletcher: "She is an avid runner, mother, and teacher. She qualified for the Boston Marathon. You can't teach, raise children, and train all during regular business hours. She is a phenomenal amazing woman who needs our help, not any judgment."

**3. Fletcher Showcased Pictures of Her Family on Social Media & Wrote About Her Love of True Crime Podcasts:** On her Facebook page, Fletcher showcased photos of her husband, Richie Fletcher, and their two young children. Her most recent post, in 2021, other than a profile picture of her family, reads, “Need a new general practitioner. Can someone recommend a good, easy-to-get appointment for Dr or NP?” Fletcher’s Facebook posts were about mundane activities. “I need tv show recommendations...? I’m up for older shows or newer ones,” read one. In one post, though, she told her friends she was looking for a new true-crime podcast. She also wrote about running: “Long distance runners, what do you think is the best form of cross training?” She wrote, “Best podcasts to listen to while running. I liked serial, up and vanished, and dr death. I enjoy the happy hour and I’ll have another.” Her Instagram page is filled with photos of her husband and kids, biking, family trips, and so forth. She wrote recently on Instagram, The boys woke me with handmade cards, balloons, and breakfast. I love my family. I am an imperfect mother. Every day I am working to move from rigidity to flexibility, shame to grace, perfection, and criticism to acceptance and gratefulness. I want to be a mom that is a safe place for the boys to feel, be themselves and fail while learning. As a raise these boys I am reteaching my inner child at the same time. Gotta shout out to @fletch_livves who go through this process with me and loves me at the same time. #surrender @fletch_livves is the Instagram page of her husband, Richie Fletcher, a long-distance bicycle rider. In March, he wrote on Instagram, "8 years in the making with this smoking hot babe! Wouldn't want it any other way."

**4. Fletcher Is From a Well-Known Memphis Family & Is Active in Church:** According to the Commercial Appeal, Fletcher is from a well-known family in Memphis. She is "the granddaughter of the late Joseph 'Joe' Orgill III," described by the publication as a "Memphis hardware businessman and philanthropist who has supported causes including Dixon Gallery and Gardens and Church Health."

Orgill's obituary says he left behind nine grandchildren at the time of his death. She married Richard Fletcher III in 2014, Memphis Magazine reported. That article described the nuptials as a "Memorable Memphis Wedding." Richard Fletcher III is also called Richie Fletcher. The magazine described Fletcher as "a 'natural' girl – outdoorsy, athletic and warm – and the plans for her wedding emanated from her personality and style." The story noted that Fletcher's parents, "Adele and Beasley Wellford, were happy to be able to give their daughter the woodland-themed wedding she envisioned."

The story continued, "The wedding ceremony was held at nearby Second Presbyterian Church, which was indeed where the happy couple met; the officiant was Reverend Mitchell Moore. Echoing the naturalistic theme, Liza's elegant wedding gown by Austin Scarlett was painted with pale mauve flowers." George Robertson, the senior pastor at Second Presbyterian Church, told the Commercial Appeal, "She and her husband Ritchie are both very active and great leaders in our congregation. They have two little boys who have come up to me every week and hug me."

**5. There Was a Sudden Flurry of Law Enforcement Activity in the Case on Sunday Night, September 3, 2022:** On Saturday, September 3, 2022, there was a sudden flurry of activity in the case. Memphis police tweeted, "UPDATE: the vehicle of interest has been located and a male who was occupying the vehicle has been detained. Eliza Fletcher has not been located. This is an ongoing investigation. Anyone with information should call CrimeStoppers at 901-528-CASH." According to ABC24, the SUV crashed into an ATF vehicle. A woman who lives in the apartment complex near where the SUV was found posted photos showing crime scene tape around the grounds and a pond and wrote, "...It's yellow tape EVERYWHERE... now it's 2 tow trucks and ambulance over here." Social media comments indicated the apartment complex is called Lakes at Ridgeway and is about 15-20 minutes from the abduction scene.

There was a massive law enforcement presence at the Memphis apartment complex. A woman shared photos showing crime scene tape near a Family Dollar and McDonald's restaurant and claimed a McDonald's employee told them clothes were found in a dumpster. However, authorities have not confirmed the latter information. ABC24 journalist Ian Ripple tweeted photos from that scene, writing, "Now there is a large police presence at this shopping center a few miles from the apartment complex where a vehicle matching the description was towed. Can't confirm a relation to the #ElizaFletcher investigation. Some of these officers were also searching Overton Park last night."

# CHAPTER 3

## *What's New?*

Fletcher's disappearance sparked an intense hunt buoyed by surveillance video that police said showed her being forced into an SUV early Friday while she was on a jog -- that led to Henderson's arrest near his Memphis home Saturday. Fletcher's body was found near a vacant duplex Monday, and was publicly identified Tuesday, authorities said. The teacher's death, which authorities say was violent, has reverberated around the Tennessee city and still is surrounded by questions about where and how she was killed and why. Still, investigators "have no reason to think this was anything other than an isolated attack by a stranger," Mulroy told reporters Tuesday. As the investigation unfolds, Fletcher's community is mourning the junior kindergarten teacher and mother of two. She was "a joy to everyone who knew her," her family said in a statement obtained by CNN affiliate WHBQ.

We are heartbroken and devastated by this senseless loss. Liza was such a joy to so many, her family, friends, colleagues, students, parents, members of her Second Presbyterian Church congregation, and everyone who knew her," the statement reads. Now it's time to remember and celebrate how special she was and to support those who cared so much for her. We appreciate all the expressions of love and concern we have received. We are grateful beyond measure to local, state, and federal law enforcement for their tireless efforts to find Liza and to bring justice to the person responsible for this horrible crime, Fletcher's family said. At St. Mary's Episcopal School, the faculty and staff started the day in the chapel and lit candles in Fletcher's memory, the school said Tuesday in a Facebook post.

We are heartbroken at the loss of our beloved teacher, colleague, and friend Liza Fletcher, the St. Mary's Episcopal School said. More than 1,700 runners have signed up to honor her on Friday by doing an 8.2-mile route like the one she would regularly run, according to organizers. Our goal is to stand up for the women in the Mid South and emphasize that women should be able to safely run any time of day," they wrote on Facebook.

Henderson, 38, was arraigned Tuesday on the initial charges especially aggravated kidnapping and tampering with evidence and at the time was appointed a public defender to represent him. Police also analyzed a pair of sandals that were found at the abduction site, near the victim's phone. DNA found on the shoes matched Henderson's DNA, the affidavit reads. Investigators interviewed Henderson's employer, who said he drove a GMC Terrain and verified his phone number.

Investigators checked Henderson's cell phone records, which showed he was near the abduction scene during the time of Fletcher's kidnapping, according to the affidavit. Members of a US Marshals task force found a GMC Terrain near Henderson's home on Saturday morning and it had the same distinguishable damage seen in the surveillance footage, and the license plate matched the partial plate information gleaned from the video, the affidavit reads. The task force detained Henderson near his home Saturday, the court document said. Police gathered details from two witnesses including Henderson's brother who says they saw him acting strangely at the brother's Memphis house after the abduction, according to the affidavit. Both said Henderson cleaned the interior of the GMC Terrain with floor cleaner, and that he washed his clothes in the sink of the home, according to the affidavit. Cleotha Henderson, right, faces forward during a hearing in a Shelby County courtroom Wednesday.

The suspect served prison time in the previous kidnapping case

Court records also reveal that Henderson previously served a prison sentence for an aggravated kidnapping more than 20 years ago. In November 2001, Henderson pleaded guilty to the charge and was released in November 2020, court records show. Henderson had been convicted in the kidnapping of an attorney in 2000, the Shelby County district attorney's office told local outlet WREG. This month, Henderson also is facing charges unrelated to Fletcher's case, including identity theft, theft of property $1,000 or less, and fraudulent use/illegal possession of a credit or debit card $1,000 or less, Shelby County jail records show. Those charges are connected to a theft report filed last week by a woman who reported someone was using her Cash App card and Wisely Card at gas stations without her knowledge.

www.ingramcontent.com/pod-product-compliance
Lightning Source LLC
LaVergne TN
LVHW052110160826
845678LV00015B/3460

* 9 7 9 8 3 5 1 7 5 6 1 5 8 *